FINDING
THE SUN

BY EDWARD ALBEE

★

★

DRAMATISTS
PLAY SERVICE
INC.

SPECIAL NOTE

AUTHOR'S NOTE

Finding the Sun was written (and copyright) in 1983, to satisfy a commission from the University of Northern Colorado. It was first performed there that year, directed by the author (me). It was subsequently performed at the University of California-Irvine (same director) and at the University of Houston (ibid).

I was making plans for a New York production of the play in 1987 when Tina Howe's *Coastal Disturbances* (written or at least copyrighted in 1987) opened off-Broadway. By bizarre coincidence, Miss Howe's play shares a beach setting with *Finding the Sun,* a not dissimilar group of characters and — inevitably — some of the same general preoccupations.

Gut instinct told me that while the two plays were independent conceptions Miss Howe's had occupied the field — or the beach, to be more exact — and, should mine be then presented some cloudy journalistic minds would deduce that the earlier play (mine) had been substantially influenced by the later one (Miss Howe's).

Life is tough enough these days without any of that nonsense, so I have postponed New York production of *Finding the Sun* for a while, at least until the sea air clears.

I publish it with pleasure, however, for I am quite proud of it; further, with both texts now available the interested play reader will discover that Miss Howe's play and mine are, in the end, quite different matters.

CHARACTERS

ABIGAIL — twenty-three; mousy brown/blond hair, pinched features; not tall; thinnish; not pretty, but not plain.

BENJAMIN— thirty; blond, willowy-handsome; medium height.

CORDELIA — twenty-eight; attractive in a cold way; dark or raven hair; tallish; good figure.

DANIEL — thirty-seven; dark; tall; good-looking.

EDMEE — Forty-five, or so; smallish; a together, stylish matron.

FERGUS — Sixteen; blond, handsome healthy kid; swimmer's body.

GERTRUDE — Sixty; small, gray hair, deeply tanned, thinnish, elegant outdoors woman.

HENDEN — Seventy; big, sprawly man; white hair; looks like a retired diplomat.

SETTING

A beach in bright sun. Eight beach chairs — candy striped or of various colors — spread about, leaving a free area downstage center. A narrow boardwalk upstage with railing.

LIGHT

Bright sun; August, a New England day. Toward the end of the play, a lighting shift; until then, still sun.

COSTUMES

Whatever beach outfits seem most appropriate to each of the characters and the actors playing them. Towels, bags, and the usual beach stuff as well.

AUTHOR'S NOTE

The scenes of the play flow into one another without pause, although a tiny "breath" between them — more a new upbeat than anything else — would be nice.

FINDING
THE SUN

SCENE 1

Rise from black; hold for two seconds. Abigail and Benjamin enter; bathing suits, beach stuff.

ABIGAIL. *(Stretching.)* Ah! Find the sun!

BENJAMIN. *(Nods; pleased approval.)* Find the sun! *(They begin setting up. Cordelia and Daniel enter; bathing suits, beach stuff. They do not see Abigail or Benjamin, nor do they see these two.)*

CORDELIA. Find the sun, you said. *(Smiles, stretches.)*

DANIEL. *(Abstracted smile.)* Did I? "Find the sun?" Well? So? *(They begin setting up. Edmee and Fergus enter; same action as above.)*

EDMEE. Finding the sun should always be your first action, Fergus.

FERGUS. *(Feigned puzzlement.)* Not finding a chair with your back to the wall?

EDMEE. *(Happy with it.)* Outdoors ... the sun. *(Looks about.)* Goodness, look at all the people!

FERGUS. *(Mock concern.)* Gosh, Mother, will we never be alone!?

EDMEE. *(Throaty chuckle.)* Oh, hush! *(They begin setting up. Gertrude and Henden enter; same procedures as others.)*

GERTRUDE. Oh, Henden! We've found the sun!

HENDEN. We've found what? Oh! The sun! *(Sighs.)* You're right: we've found the sun. *(Pause.)*

ALL. *(Settling in.)* Ahhhhhhhhh!

SCENE 2

Daniel rises, moves D.R.; Benjamin sees him, moves to him; Abigail has her eyes closed, as does Cordelia.

BENJAMIN. Is that you!? It is! It's you!
DANIEL. I *thought* it was.
BENJAMIN. *(Sotto voce.)* What are you *doing* here?
DANIEL. ... though I remember saying to Cordelia — in the car — do you think that's me?
BENJAMIN. I mean, I was sitting there and there you were!
DANIEL. *(Quick, mirthless smile.)* Seems like old times.
BENJAMIN. *(Blurting on.)* Are you here alone? I mean, are you with Cordelia?
DANIEL. No: I'm here with a couple of tricks named Jeremy and Phillip I picked up in ...
BENJAMIN. *(Shy smile.)* Oh, come on, Daniel.
DANIEL. *(Mimicking.)* Oh, come on, Benjie-wengie!
BENJAMIN. *(After a tiny pause.)* So many people here.
DANIEL. *(A hand on Benjamin's shoulder.)* I miss you.
BENJAMIN. *(Shrugs; smiles.)* I *love* you.
DANIEL. *(Nods; removes his hand.)* I love you, *and* I *miss* you.
BENJAMIN. *(Giggles.)* I wonder what Abigail will say.
DANIEL. Abigail will say ...
ABIGAIL. *(Seeing Benjamin gone.)* Benjamin!? Where are you!?
DANIEL. *That* is what Abigail will say.

SCENE 3

Benjamin and Daniel move back to their places as Edmee and Fergus move D.L.

EDMEE. *(As they come.)* Having found the sun — the good sun, the clear, healing heat — having *found* the sun, *then* you put your back to the wall.
FERGUS. *(Imitation of eager student.)* Aha!

EDMEE. The sun is the source of all life: the aminos and all the rest couldn't have done their work with*out* it, you see.
FERGUS. A*ha!!*
EDMEE. Look at your civilizations! Africa! — if you call that a civilization — four? five million years ago, in the hottest of the muck, down there, closest to boiling, the *cradle* of it.
FERGUS. *We* live in New Hampshire.
EDMEE. *(Ignoring? Not having heard?)* And the Mediterranean basin? Greece? Rome? The Parthenon is *not* in Bergin, Norway, my dear. *(Peering.)* I wonder who those people are? Nor does the Appian Way run through Tierra del Fuego.
FERGUS. Nor New Hampshire.
EDMEE. *(Not angry.)* Be civil.
FERGUS. Oh, Mother!
EDMEE. Everything proceeds comparatively, it is true — there is no light without dark, rest without action, and so forth and so on — and a life in the tropics produces a ... lassitude which leads to an absence of philosophical inquiry, but nor have the Lapps or the Eskimos given us much beyond some charming little carvings — doo-dads, really; no, time in the sun *and* time away: that's the ticket! Everything comparative; everything in season.
FERGUS. Okay.
EDMEE. Why do you dwell on New Hampshire?
FERGUS. We dwell *in* New Hampshire.
EDMEE. You dwell in your own skin. Do you dwell on that?
FERGUS. A life of acne?
EDMEE. This, too, shall pass. *(Sees Gertrude rising, coming toward them.)* Is that lady coming to talk to us?
FERGUS. *(Rising.)* To you.
EDMEE. *(Sincerely bothered.)* Oh, Fergus! Maybe you'll like her.
FERGUS. *(Moving away.)* Let me know. *(Nods to the approaching Gertrude.)* Ma'am.
GERTRUDE. *(Nods.)* Young man. *(To Edmee.)* Is that yours?
EDMEE. Yes; yes, he is.
GERTRUDE. What is he to you, or am I being nosy?
EDMEE. I beg your pardon? Yes, you probably are.

GERTRUDE. I *always* am. I can't help myself.

EDMEE. *(To get it straight.)* What *is* he to me?

GERTRUDE. Henden says to me, you are the nosiest woman in Christendom, and this in spite of that little gouge above the left nostril, that little gouge where they took the cancer off. Would you believe that I've had four skin cancers removed — all from the sun! — and I still won't stay out of it? Don't go in the sun, Gertrude: You know your propensities.

EDMEE. What *is* he to me? Who is Henden?

GERTRUDE. Or, more to the point, who is *Sylvia?* Henden is my husband, my third; the other two I lost — not through carelessness, but time: I marry older men. Henden is the youngest I have married — in distance from *my* age, I mean to say. Henden is only seventy. What is he to *you;* well, what *is* he to you? — the young boy: Is he your son, your nephew, your ward your ... lover?

EDMEE. *(A smile.)* You *should* stay out of the sun.

SCENE 4

Edmee and Gertrude stay where they are, Gertrude having sat in Fergus's chair. Abigail and Cordelia come D.R.

ABIGAIL. He's such a child; he behaves like ... such a child!

CORDELIA. *(Eyes closed; absorbing the sun.)* Hmmmmmmmmm-mmm.

ABIGAIL. He comes back — when I call him — he comes back, plops himself down in in his chair, and starts blathering on about ... all the *sail*boats, there are *no* clouds, *are* there!, *where* will we go for dinner ...

CORDELIA. Hmmmmmmmmmmmm.

ABIGAIL. Not a word! Not one word about running into Daniel ...

CORDELIA. Hmmmmmmmmmmmm.

ABIGAIL. ... which meant, naturally, that *you* were here,

which information was of interest to *me*....

CORDELIA.   Hmmmmmmmmmmmm.

ABIGAIL.   Not a word!

CORDELIA.   *(Stretching; drawled.)* Well, what would you expect?

ABIGAIL.   You would think....

CORDELIA.   What do you *really expect?*

ABIGAIL.   *(Too brightly innocent.)* I beg your pardon?

CORDELIA.   I know them both as well as you know Benjamin — better, probably. Recall I knew them *before* you, and they were *lovers* then....

ABIGAIL.   *(Too bright.)* Well, they're not lovers now!

CORDELIA.   Because they married us, you mean? Remember the leopard.

ABIGAIL.   I beg your pardon?

CORDELIA.   Do you not *like* me — or are you like that, I mean ... naturally?

ABIGAIL.   *(Abrupt laugh.)* Whatever do you mean?

CORDELIA.   Your tone, baby.

ABIGAIL.   *(Haughty.)* I have no idea what you mean.

CORDELIA.   Okay. Just remember the leopard.

ABIGAIL.   I'm supposed to understand what that means?

CORDELIA.   *Are* you retarded? Leopard! Leopard: spots. A leopard doesn't change its spots.

ABIGAIL.   *(Snooty.)* I can't speak for you and Daniel, but Benjamin is home with me every night.

CORDELIA.   *(Dry.)* How *nice* for him.

ABIGAIL.   *(Pleased; proud.)* I never let him out of my sight.

CORDELIA.   They must love you in the men's rooms.

ABIGAIL.   *(Riding over that.)* You and Daniel may have what is referred to as an "arrangement" — by which is usually implied a moral quagmire — and, to be sure, Daniel may not have ... adjusted to the world, but Benjamin has seen the follies of his ways, his *former* ways, and ...

CORDELIA.   Oh, bullshit! *(Abigail fumes, moves away.)*

9

SCENE 5

Henden puttering, Fergus coming upon him.

FERGUS. Hello.

HENDEN. Hello.

FERGUS. How old are you?

HENDEN. What an odd question! I'm seventy.

FERGUS. That's what I thought: you're the oldest person here — in the vicinity.

HENDEN. I often am.

FERGUS. And I'm the youngest. I'm sixteen.

HENDEN. Don't be silly.

FERGUS. A lot of people say that.

HENDEN. There is no such age.

FERGUS. Yes, that's what they say. Why are you here?

HENDEN. Why am I *anywhere!?* Luck, I guess; or that's what they call it.

FERGUS. Who do *you* belong with?

HENDEN. *Again* such an odd question! I am *with* my wife, my Gertrude, the one was talking with the lady you arrived with, I believe; that is who I am *with.* As to whether it is Gertrude I *belong* with ... well, that would take some mulling.

FERGUS. Mull away.

HENDEN. By which I mean — thank you ...

FERGUS. You're welcome.

HENDEN. ... by which I mean that I am very fond of Gertrude, as wives go — though I've had only two — but whether it is she I *belong* with ... well, that takes some pondering.

FERGUS. What happened to the first one?

HENDEN. *(Shrugs.)* She died; after forty-six years of marriage with me she took it into her head to die.

FERGUS. Literally?

HENDEN. Yes; a brain tumor.

FERGUS. Forty-six years is a very long time. *(Afterthought.)* Sorry.

HENDEN.   Not in retrospect: only during. And I married
Gertrude — though I like her very much — I suppose to *be
married,* as much as anything: a continuity.
FERGUS.   Hmmmm. I suspect I'm a little young for a sense
of continuity.   There's a theory afoot, though, that we young
and we old have things in common should bind us together
against those in the middle.
HENDEN.   Heavens! And what *are* those things?
FERGUS.   I haven't the faintest. Doesn't anybody swim
around here?
HENDEN.   The beginning and the end! An alliance! Well,
maybe; might work as well as most. Who do *you* belong with?
FERGUS.   Well, I'm here with my mother — the lady your
Gertrude was talking with — and since I *am* only sixteen and
I legally belong *to* her, I daresay I belong *with* her. The day
will come, though ... well, the day will come. Who *are* all
these people!?
HENDEN.   Well, we've accounted for the two of *us,* for
Gertrude and your mother; that leaves the other four.
FERGUS.   ... of those nearby.
HENDEN.   Well, surely I'm not to account for the entire
coast. The couple over *there (Indicates Cordelia and Daniel.)* are
Daniel and Cordelia; Daniel is my son — by my first mar-
riage, of course; his wife, Cordelia, is daughter to Gertrude —
by one of *her* earliers.
FERGUS.   My goodness! You know everything! Who are the
others? Do you know?
HENDEN.   The other couple? Abigail and Benjamin.
FERGUS.   Heaven, you do! Whose daughter and son are
they!?
HENDEN.   No one's — well, someone's, naturally, but none
of ours.
FERGUS.   Strangers!
HENDEN.   Not exactly. Well, perhaps, though they *are* mar-
ried — to each other! No, the cord binding them to us is, uh
.... a complex twine.
FERGUS.   We've heard of that in New Hampshire, I believe.
HENDEN.   Abigail did not exist before she married Ben-

jamin, but Benjamin ... well, he and Daniel, before Daniel married Cordelia, he and Daniel were ... well, how shall I put it...?

FERGUS. I don't know!

HENDEN. ... were ... involved.

FERGUS. I beg your pardon?

HENDEN. Benjamin and Daniel were "involved."

FERGUS. *(Trying to sort it out.)* With one another.

HENDEN. Yes.

FERGUS. In a business sense?

HENDEN. How old are you?

FERGUS. Sixteen — but I'm from New Hampshire.

HENDEN. *(Understanding.)* Of course. No; in a ... personal sense.

FERGUS. Yes?

HENDEN. Benjamin and Daniel were lovers.

FERGUS. *(Long pause.)* With each other?

HENDEN. Yes.

FERGUS. My goodness. *(Considers.)* I believe we've heard of this in New Hampshire. They loved one another?

HENDEN. Certainly.

FERGUS. And gave each other physical pleasure.

HENDEN. As I understand it.

FERGUS. Why are they no longer lovers? Pleasure into pain?

HENDEN. *(Slightly standoffish.)* You'll have to ask them that, young man.

FERGUS. Well, I shall! *(Afterthought.)* I've not been lovers with *anyone.*

HENDEN. Well, you're sixteen.

FERGUS. Romeo was fifteen, they say, but he was Italian.

HENDEN. When you're older....

FERGUS. My hand and I will say good-bye?

HENDEN. Well, will probably develop a more casual relationship.

FERGUS. Oh? Pity.

HENDEN. If you *do* speak to Daniel or Benjamin of their ... liaison ...

FERGUS. Yes?

12

HENDEN. *Do* be cautious.

FERGUS. Oh?

HENDEN. Well, you *are* very young and very ...

FERGUS. *(Contemptuous.)* Pretty?

HENDEN. *(Gently.)* I was going to say "handsome."

FERGUS. *(Melting.)* Thank you!

HENDEN. But you are ... young.

FERGUS. That's very true, sir, but don't forget that I'm ...

HENDEN. *(A hand up.)* I know! You're from New Hampshire.

SCENE 6

Henden moves U.; Fergus crosses to Edmee and Gertrude.

FERGUS. *(Moving by fast; to Edmee.)* Have I got things to tell *you!*

GERTRUDE. *(After Fergus goes.)* Who *is* that?

EDMEE. *(Pause.)* What?

SCENE 7

Cordelia and Daniel together.

CORDELIA. I was *so terrible* to Abigail!

DANIEL. *(Reading? Sunning?)* That's nice.

CORDELIA. Do you know what I think it is?

DANIEL. *(Ibid.)* Hmmmm?

CORDELIA. Do you know why I think I'm so terrible to Abigail?

DANIEL. *(Becoming involved.)* Well, let's see: Because she's here? because you don't like her? because she's turning Benjamin into a shell — sucking him dry, you should excuse the expression? because she's a self-obsessed, tedious bore of a woman?

13

CORDELIA.   *(Considers it.)* *Those* are interesting.

DANIEL.   *I* thought so.

CORDELIA.   But no; I think I'm terrible to her because there she is with Benjamin and I loathe Benjamin and she *doesn't* control him in *spite* of your lies....

DANIEL.   You don't loathe Benjamin.

CORDELIA.   The two of you are as close now as you ever were....

DANIEL.   What did you do — you and Miss Abbey — marry us as part of a sisterhood solidarity reform movement? And you're falling out among yourselves? You never told me any of this; you should choose your co-conspirators better.

CORDELIA.   *(Not to be put off.)* The two of you are as close now as you ever were — which I will probably divorce you for one day....

DANIEL.   *(Harsh laugh.)* You wouldn't dare! Your family'd kill you over the publicity: famous former deb, mainline family heirloom — heiress, sorry! — married to fag, files for annulment, names hubby's former hubby as ...

CORDELIA.   The two of you are as close now as you ever were — which I will probably divorce you for one day — and I'm probably taking *that* out on poor Abigail.

DANIEL.   Plus you don't like her.

CORDELIA.   Why doesn't she make Benjamin take her to live in Peru, or somewhere?

DANIEL.   Because, pussycat, then *we'd* have to move to Peru, too, and you *know* how you are with languages....

CORDELIA.   Why doesn't she ... *(Stops.)*

DANIEL.   Yes; why doesn't she!

CORDELIA.   *(Giggles.)* I accused her of following Benjamin into men's rooms!

DANIEL.   *(Giggles.)* You're not *nice!*

CORDELIA.   *(Hand out to him; after a beat.)* What *are* we to do?

DANIEL.   *(Takes her hand.)* Give it some time.

CORDELIA.   It's been three years.

DANIEL.   Give it some *time.*

CORDELIA.   *Do* you see him secretly?

DANIEL. *(Pause.)* No.
CORDELIA. Do you see *anyone?*
DANIEL. *(Gently.)* Don't probe.
CORDELIA. I love you, you see.
DANIEL. And I love you. *(Pause.)* I've got a very roomy heart. *(Pause; then she begins to laugh; he, too.)*

SCENE 8

Cordelia and Daniel return to their books, or whatever.

EDMEE. *(Turning to Gertrude both still in their beach chairs. Very casual, informal, informational.)* Well, now, to answer your question — your pry, to be more accurate, about Fergus. What he *is* to me is too much. He is my son — he *is:* real mother, real son. And since my husband died — his father — he has been the "man" in my life, so to speak. It's four years now since his father dove off the rocks — showing off, as usual — hit some jutting something underwater wasn't supposed to be there, broke his neck, drowned. *(Shrugs.)* These things happen. I haven't thought of remarrying; perhaps I will, later. I've raised Fergus; he's a good boy. There is, I think — there may be — an attachment transcends the usual, the socially *admitted* usual, that is, by which I mean: given the provocation, Fergus would bed me in a moment. A mother knows these things, even admits knowing them.... Sometimes. He doesn't know it, or, if he *does* sense it, is polite or shrewd enough to pretend he does *not*. It is more usual for a son to lust after his mother than a mother for her son, so there is little surprise in the information that my interest in bedding Fergus is minimal. I mean, God! I have birthed him, I have held him, rocked him, comforted him, bathed him, scolded him, dressed him, guided him ... why on earth would I want to fuck him!? *(Gertrude drops whatever she is holding.)*

SCENE 9

Edmee and Gertrude stay where they are; focus on Abigail and Benjamin.

ABIGAIL. Cordelia doesn't like me!

BENJAMIN. *(Taking the sun; eyes shut.)* Ohhhhhhh ...

ABIGAIL. You know perfectly well she doesn't!

BENJAMIN. Well ...

ABIGAIL. Why don't you tell Daniel to *make* her like me!?

BENJAMIN. Oh, I don't think I ...

ABIGAIL. Certainly it would make everything easier. I mean, if we're going to live in this proximity, with all the strings and all ...

BENJAMIN. *(Eyes open.)* Oh, God!

ABIGAIL. ... having her like me, or at least making a good stab at *pretending* to like me, would be a help. *You* don't help.

BENJAMIN. Oh, God!

ABIGAIL. Nor does "Oh, God" help.

BENJAMIN. Oh, God!

ABIGAIL. You and your sidelong glances, your letters you won't let me read, your odd phone calls, your feeble excuses for getting home late, your ...

BENJAMIN. *(Rises.)* Oh, God! *(Leaves her area.)*

ABIGAIL. *(Genuine surprise.)* Where are you going?

SCENE 10

Henden comes D.F.

HENDEN. *(To the audience.)* I get frightened sometimes. Don't you? About dying, I mean? What is the age we become aware of it? That we *know* it's going to happen, even if we don't accept it? It differs with the person, I'm told. The earlier on the better — well, no: I don't mean that young man

16

over there; I don't mean *he* should be burdened with it, not at *his* age, but somewhere in the thirties — forties at the ... most tardy — it will come on healthy little feet; much later and you're whistling in the ... light, I suppose. When you reach *my* age you ... well, you get a little frightened sometimes. Because you're alone. Oh? Really? Wife, if you're lucky? Children? *Grand*children? Yes, certainly, if you're lucky, but you're still ... alone. *(Taps his head.)* Nobody gets in there with you. Greek peasants have a room they keep their coffin in, ready for the day. *(Shrugs.)* No difference there from keeping it in the back of your head, the back of your mind. Being seventy gives me a few more years, if we're to believe the actuaries — three, four. That's a help, though it isn't a guarantee, and I feel pretty well. Oh ... I have the usual: one hip not so hot; arthritis in the neck; something uncomfortable down in my lower gut, fairly steadily; a little ... loss of sensation in my left arm now and again, and I fainted once, last week, tieing my shoes. *(Shrugs.)* The usual. I go to my doctor once every year or so. I ask him; he says, "You're getting old!" Well, I *am*. Still. Nothing to be done about it, but I *do* get ... just a little ... frightened now and again. Being alive is ... so splendid. *(Smiles.)* Ah, well. *(Move back to his beach chair.)*

SCENE 11

Benjamin moves to where Daniel and Cordelia are sunning.

BENJAMIN.   I can't stand it! Can I move in with you two?
DANIEL.   *May* I.
BENJAMIN.   *May* I? *May* I move in with you two?
CORDELIA.   No.
DANIEL.   No.
BENJAMIN.   *(A whine.)* Whhhhhyyyy?
CORDELIA.   Just because.
BENJAMIN.   Aw, come on, guys!
CORDELIA.   You made your bed, now sleep in it.

17

DANIEL.   Besides, we *have* someone moving in.

CORDELIA.   *(After the briefest catching-on pause.)* Yes; yes, we have.

BENJAMIN.   *(Mistrustful.)* Who?

CORDELIA.   Well ... *(Looks to Daniel.)*

DANIEL.   We wrote in to one of those magazines for swingers....

CORDELIA.   ... *Swingers Mag,* it's called....

DANIEL.   ... that's right: *Swingers Mag,* and we saw an ad in there for a bi stud wanted to relocate ...

CORDELIA.   ... six foot seven, two hundred and thirty-five pounds, wrestler's body ...

DANIEL.   ... goes both ways, into three-scenes or solos, fully reciprocal, light S and M, no femmes or fatties.

CORDELIA.   It seemed like a perfect addition to the house: cheaper than a new playroom, or ...

DANIEL.   He gets here tomorrow; we paid his way, of course.

BENJAMIN.   *(After a brief, thinking pause.)* We could do foursies!

DANIEL.   Rub-a-dub-dub, three men and a tub?

CORDELIA.   Don't be witty.

BENJAMIN.   I don't believe you guys! You wouldn't dare!

DANIEL.   *(Haughty.)* And why not, pray?

CORDELIA.   Yes, and why not?

BENJAMIN.   Because Henden and Gertrude wouldn't put up with it. *(A silence.)*

CORDELIA.   He has a point there.

DANIEL.   Mmmmmmmmmm; afraid he has.

BENJAMIN.   They'd let *me* move in with you, though; they *like me.*

CORDELIA.   Tell you what: you go live with *them.*

DANIEL.   Right, and we'll send you a subscription to the magazine.

BENJAMIN.   *(Moving off.)* You guys are no help.

DANIEL.   *(To Cordelia.)* No help?

CORDELIA.   *(To Daniel.)* Really?

SCENE 12

Abigail and Fergus. Abigail by herself, talking to herself.

ABIGAIL.   *(Practicing.)* Benjamin, this can't go on! Benjamin?, you and I have to have a talk. Benjamin, grow up! *(Faster.)* Who do you think I am, Benjamin? Benjamin, just who do you think you are? I'm leaving you, Benjamin; No, I'll never give you a divorce, you .... you ...; you're making our lives a shambles, Benjamin; we could have been so happy together. *(Pause.)* Nuts! *(To Fergus, who is ambling by, listening, really.)* *You're* not married, *are* you.
FERGUS.   Hello!
ABIGAIL.   You're not, are you; of *course* you're not; you're ... you're an adolescent.
FERGUS.   I was going to say, my, aren't you pretty! But that word killed it.
ABIGAIL.   What word?
FERGUS.   Adolescent. If there's one thing an adolescent doesn't want to be called it's an adolescent — even those of us *know* we're adolescents, accept it, we don't want the word used: we don't like the sound of it. Ad-o-les-cent; it's an ugly word.
ABIGAIL.   I'm *sorry!*
FERGUS.   *(Comforting.)* I *know* you are; I'm *sure* of it.
ABIGAIL.   What would you *like* to be called?
FERGUS.   Fergus.
ABIGAIL.   What a .... pretty name. I meant generically.
FERGUS.   Young man?
ABIGAIL.   *(Considers it.)* Young man. That has a nice sound. *You* are a ... young man.
FERGUS.   My, aren't you pretty! There; you see? One good turn of phrase deserves another.
ABIGAIL.   I don't feel particularly pretty right now.
FERGUS.   How come?
ABIGAIL.   *(Looks about to see if anyone is listening.)* I'm ....

19

married.

FERGUS. *(Cheerful.)* I know: to the gentleman over there used to be ... involved with that other gentleman, who is ... where? Ah! Over there, with who! — his wife!

ABIGAIL. My God, you know everything, don't you. Do *all* of you know everything?

FERGUS. Who is ... all?

ABIGAIL. All is too much, most likely.

FERGUS. Have ... have you and the *other* lady been ... involved?

ABIGAIL. I beg your pardon!

FERGUS. Have you and the other lady ...

ABIGAIL. Certainly not!

FERGUS. You make it seem so ... definite.

ABIGAIL. Well, it *is!*

FERGUS. But why?

ABIGAIL. Cordelia and I are not ... that *way.*

FERGUS. I see!

ABIGAIL. *(Transparent.)* Nor are Benjamin and Daniel.

FERGUS. I see; yes, I see.

ABIGAIL. Far too much!

FERGUS. Ma'am?

ABIGAIL. Who have you been talking to? To Gertrude? To Henden? Gertrude is Cordelia's mother, you know.

FERGUS. Really?

ABIGAIL. Yes, and Henden is Daniel's father.

FERGUS. My goodness!

ABIGAIL. And Gertrude and Henden are married now.

FERGUS. Gracious!

ABIGAIL. And who's the woman you're with?

FERGUS. Edmee? She's my mother.

ABIGAIL. There's too much family on this beach. I'm the outsider.

FERGUS. *(Considers it.)* Well, that must give you a perspective.

ABIGAIL. It gives me nothing! It gives me the pip!

FERGUS. Pip is given a lot, isn't it.

ABIGAIL. Stay away from Daniel; he's dangerous. *(After-*

thought.) **For** that matter, stay away from Benjamin, too.

FERGUS. But ... why?

ABIGAIL. You're very young.

FERGUS. Where is *your* family?

ABIGAIL. They died in a collision.

FERGUS. Oh, I'm so sorry! My mother says the roads are a terrible place. *(Abigail inaudible.)* Pardon?

ABIGAIL. Not a car! Not roads!

FERGUS. An airplane!

ABIGAIL. No.

FERGUS. *(Puzzles.)* A train, then!

ABIGAIL. No.

FERGUS. *(Awe.)* Boats? *(Abigail inaudible again.)* Pardon?

ABIGAIL. Balloons.

FERGUS. *(Pause.)* Pardon?

ABIGAIL. *(Too loud.)* Balloons! *(Softer.)* Balloons.

FERGUS. My goodness.

ABIGAIL. *(Still sad and perplexed over it.)* They were in central Texas — antiquing — and they came upon a town — I don't know, *some*where — and the shops weren't any good, I guess, and they called me, very excited, and said they were going ballooning, that there was an outfit took people up for an hour ride — hot air balloons, you know?

FERGUS. I *guess.*

ABIGAIL. Be careful, I said. What can happen, they said; what are we going to run into in a hot-air balloon? You never know, I said. Tush, they said, and off they went!

FERGUS. And?

ABIGAIL. Texas is a big state.

FERGUS. Yes.

ABIGAIL. Flat.

FERGUS. Yes.

ABIGAIL. You can see for ... miles.

FERGUS. I don't doubt it. *(Pauses.)* They hit something? *(Abigail shakes her head. Awe.)* Something hit *them?* *(Abigail nods.)* My gracious!

ABIGAIL. A boy genius! Are you bright? Very bright?

FERGUS. I believe so.

ABIGAIL.   Damn your eyes! A boy genius, building his own rocket — out in all that flatness — building his very own rocket. You'd think he would *see* something in all that flatness, wouldn't you? Sets the fucking thing off — on its way to Mars, I suppose — and it goes right through the bag of the balloon, and the bag deflates, and down like a shot it goes with my appalled mother and father, back to the flat, flat earth, fast, inexplicably ... and *Splat!*
FERGUS.   Oh, dear; oh, dear.
ABIGAIL.   *(Controlled.)* I went down — grief and disbelief; the boy genius had such thick glasses — prisms; enormous hands on such a slight boy; enormous hands and these .... prisms. He said he was sorry. *(A sudden explosion of tears.)* And I have to be married to a fairy! *(She runs off.)*
FERGUS.   *(To her retreating form.)* Yes ... well ... *(To himself.)* My goodness.

SCENE 13

FERGUS.   *(Comes forward; speaks to the audience.)* If you think it's easy being my age, well ... you have another think coming, as they say. A New England boyhood isn't *all* peaches and cream, maple syrup and russet autumns. I know it *sounds* pretty good — wealthy mother and all, private school, WASP education. ASP, to be precise. *Are* there any black Anglo-Saxons? It all sounds pretty nice, and it *is.* I'm not complaining; it's nice ... but it isn't always easy. Being corrupted, for example; now, that's important to a young fellow. Whether he takes advantage of it or not. The corrupting influences really should *be* there; all you should have to do is turn a corner and there you are, all laid out for you, so to speak — fornication, drugs, stealing, whatever; it should *be* there. But if you live in Grovers Corners, or wherever, pop. fifteen hundred and thirty-three, it isn't too easy to come by. You have to ... search it out. Oh, there's the grocer's youngish widow with her blinds always drawn and the come-hither look, and the mildly retarded girl in the ninth grade has some habits would make a pro blush, *and* the florist with the dyed hair and the funny walk and the mustache for those inclined that way, or at least want to try it. These things are to be *had* in a small town, but not without the peril of observation and revelation. What's missing, I suppose, is ... anonymity. And there are, after all, some things we'd rather do in private — at least until we're practiced — do them well. The lack of anonymity: Well, in a small New England town, if your family's been there eight hundred years, or whatever, and you're "gentry," *and* you're bright, *and* your mother practically sends out announcements *saying* you're bright and destined for "great things," well, then ... it's not the same, the nice same, as being able to get it all together behind the barn, so to speak, and then coming out all rehearsed and "ready." "I hear you're getting all A's, Fergus; good for you!" "Your mother says you've decided on Harvard, young fella; well, I hope they've decided on you, ha, ha, ha!" Lordy! Even when I was tiny: "Took his first step, did he!?" "Potty trained is he? Good for him!" Royalty must have it worse, or the children of the very famous. I don't even know what I want to *do* with my life — if I want to do *anything.* If I want to *live* it, even. Do you know what suicide rate has been making the biggest jumps? Kids. Kids my age. I'm not planning to ... kill myself or anything; don't misunderstand me; I'm happy, relatively happy, as I understand the term. It's just that ... well, we kids have all sorts of options. You grown-ups aren't the only ones. Think about *that.* Thank you. *(Bows, moves off.)*

SCENE 14

CORDELIA. *(Comes forward; alone. To the audience.)* I would imagine you've been wondering why I married Daniel, considering everything — Benjamin, I mean. I would imagine you've been wondering; heaven knows, *I* have, now and again. My mother — Gertrude, over there — said to me — how many times? — "Why are you *marrying* that person? I warn you, young woman, you're in for a lot of woe." "Oh, Mother," I'd say, knowing full well what she meant. "I warn you: they don't change; you'll find out!" "Oh, Mother!" Back and forth; Ping-Pong. "I had a cousin married one." "Oh, Mother!" "Scandals; driven from one town to another." "Oh God.!" "Mark my words."

GERTRUDE. *(From where she sits.)* Mark my words!

CORDELIA. *(Out.)* I married him because I love him. Doesn't that seem simple enough? We met; I found him handsome — in his way; sexy — in his way; plus bright plus tender and considerate plus patient plus he cheered me up a lot. I don't mean to suggest that I was greatly in *need* of cheering up; I'm not a manic depressive, or anything. I've had some laughs, some kicks; I've been around — married once before, to a jock, on his way to nowhere as it turned out. I've been around; I know the scene, the score, whatever. But Daniel was special — *is*. I knew he was gay — right off; some women sense these things; others never get the hang of it. I knew he was gay; I knew he and Benjamin were lovers; and I knew I wanted to marry him. *(Shrugs.)* Well, I'm a grown-up.

GERTRUDE. *(From where she sits.)* Mark my words!

CORDELIA. Oh, Mother! *(Out.)* I knew what the problems would be — *are*. I knew the chances. I *know* Daniel sleeps around; well, I'm pretty sure I know it, and I suspect it's with guys. I *hope* it is: I mean, I *like* being his only woman. I mean, if I turn him straight ... then he'll start in with girls. This way's better. As long as he's careful; as long as he's very careful.

GERTRUDE. *(From where she sits.)* You're in for a lot of woe! Mark my words!

CORDELIA. *(Laughs.)* Oh, Mother! *(Out.)* Every time we're done making love and we have our cigarettes, Daniel'll turn to me and smile and take my hand and say, "Isn't it nice that we're such good friends." Well, I suppose that isn't *exactly* your usual marriage, isn't precisely *(Imitation of jock.)* "Hey, babe, that was good for me; was it good for you, too?" Not exactly that, but *I* don't mind. I think I prefer it. I think ... I think perhaps Daniel is more interested in our friendship than our marriage. I mean, he seems ... happy enough being married to me, certainly no less happy than when he was — married, I suppose, to Benjamin. And if I lose anything, it won't be the way your usual marriage ends — the friendship goes first, and *then* the marriage falls apart. What I mean is, I think I have a friend, and if one day he thinks that our being married is as silly as it *is* ... well, then I'll lose the marriage, but I think I'll still have a very good friend. *(Shrugs.)* There are worse things in the world to have.

SCENE 15

Benjamin, Daniel, Fergus. Benjamin and Daniel are standing, separate, stretching. Fergus comes up.

FERGUS. Let's play catch.

DANIEL. I *beg* your pardon!

FERGUS. Let's play *catch.* Here; I have a ball. *(Throws and catches a beach ball.)*

BENJAMIN. Hey! Why not?

DANIEL. Why *not?* You? Catch something? Herpes is about the only thing you can catch — apparently.

FERGUS. Who's that? May we play?

BENJAMIN. Okay! Okay!

DANIEL. *(To Benjamin.)* Be sure to put your glasses on: you *do* want to catch the ball.

FERGUS. *(To Daniel.)* I'll throw it to you and you throw it to him and he'll throw it to me.

DANIEL. *(Mildly sarcastic.)* Won't this be fun!

BENJAMIN. It *will* be!

FERGUS. Okay; here we go. *(Throws at Daniel.)* Catch!

DANIEL. *(Catching.)* Ow! Jesus!

BENJAMIN. *(Parody of baseball player.)* C'mon, guy; heave her over here!

DANIEL. *(Disbelief.) Heave* her over *here?*

BENJAMIN.   Come on; have fun!

DANIEL.   Who ever heard of anybody saying anything like that? *(Underhand toss.)* Here!

BENJAMIN.   *(Sibilant comment.)* Ooooooh! My gracious! Such force!

FERGUS.   You guys are *fun! (Catches Benjamin's fair throw.)* Hey! That's good!

DANIEL.   *(Jock imitation.)* What's ya name, kid? *(Benjamin giggles; Fergus throws sort of hard to Daniel.) Ow!*

FERGUS.   Fergus. Was that too hard?

BENJAMIN.   *(Jock imitation.)* For a guy like him, kid? You kidding? *(Daniel throws very hard.)* Ow!

FERGUS.   You guys *are* fun! *(Natural, casual throwing now; unobtrusive.)*

DANIEL.   What kind of name is Fergus?

FERGUS.   Scots, I believe.

BENJAMIN.   I'm Benjamin.

FERGUS.   Hi!

DANIEL.   And I'm Lucille.

FERGUS.   *(No change in friendly tone.)* Hi!

DANIEL.   *(Awe at Fergus's aplomb.)* Wow! No, actually I'm Daniel.

FERGUS.   I know. You two are presently married to those ladies over there, although ... since the two of *you* have been ... uh ... intimately involved? ... there is a question floating around this particular area of the beach as to whether these marriages were made in heaven. I have no opinion on the matter.

BENJAMIN.   *(To Daniel; false sotto voce.)* The "in-laws" have been talking again.

FERGUS.   Are you all good friends, you four? You and your wives?

DANIEL.   It varies; it varies.

FERGUS.   I ... wondered. *(Pause.)*

BENJAMIN.   Oh?

DANIEL.   Oh?

FERGUS.   I was having a little chat with ... well, I guess *your* wife, Benjamin; uh ... Abigail is *yours?*

DANIEL. Oh, yes; Abigail is his and he is Abigail's.

BENJAMIN. Enough!

DANIEL. Desist? Hold? *Basta?*

FERGUS. You guys are really *fun!*

BENJAMIN. What *about* Abigail?

FERGUS. She's ... *(Tosses ball above his head; catches it.)* ... well, she's.... unhappy?

DANIEL. No kidding!

BENJAMIN. *(Gently.)* I *know.*

FERGUS. I'd take care if I were you.

DANIEL. *(To no one.)* What*ever* can he mean?

BENJAMIN. *(Ignoring Daniel's tone.)* Whatever *can* you mean?

FERGUS. I'd be careful of her; that's all. *(Quick subject switch.)* Which one of you guys married first?

BENJAMIN. *I* did.

FERGUS. *(Some surprise.)* Really?

DANIEL. I was planning to when this one decided to do something precipitous. "I'll show *you!*" — *that* sort of thing.

BENJAMIN. Untrue! Untrue!

DANIEL. ... when he realized that I was serious — that Cordelia and I were going to be married. When *that* sank in, he sort of ran out in the street and hooked on to the first gullible girl he could find.

BENJAMIN. Unclean! Unclean!

DANIEL. *(Naggy tone.)* "I'll show you! I'll show you!"

FERGUS. *(To Benjamin.)* I'd worry about her a little if I were you.

DANIEL. With any luck she might just ... walk out of our lives, you mean?

FERGUS. Something like that.

BENJAMIN. *(More or less to himself.)* That *is* something to think about.

FERGUS. *(Starting to leave, still tossing to himself; a kind of "Okay you guys" tone.)* Okay. Okay.

BENJAMIN. Where are you going?

DANIEL. Where are you taking the ball?

FERGUS. You guys don't need the ball; you've got your own game going. *(As Fergus leaves, a combination of regret and some-*

thing private and not too nice.)
BENJAMIN and DANIEL.   Aaaaawwwwwwwwwwww!

SCENE 16

Fergus moves behind sleeping Edmee, awakes Gertrude and Henden.

FERGUS.   Have I got things to tell *her! (Moves past, out of their view.)*
EDMEE.   *(After a pause; suddenly.)* Who *was* that?
GERTRUDE.   Your son ... or so you say.
HENDEN.   What a nice boy!
EDMEE.   My son, or so I say?
HENDEN.   Bright, too!
GERTRUDE.   I meant no offense.
EDMEE.   *(To Henden.) Very* bright. *Too* bright? — perhaps.
HENDEN.   Oh, come now!
GERTRUDE.   *(Singsong.)* No offense at all.
EDMEE.   *(Generally.)* There's danger in consciousness, in too much awareness.
HENDEN.   We go through it only once, my dear, or so more tell me than don't — better alert than ... numb, or not comprehending.
GERTRUDE.   *(To Henden; an old argument.)* You're *certain* of that — that we go *through* it only once.
HENDEN.   *(To Edmee; chuckling.)* Gertrude is of the opinion that a move away from the big bang theory to the notion that the universe has always existed, in whatever form ...
EDMEE.   *(Lazy.)* I don't believe either one.
GERTRUDE.   *(Mildly startled.)* Oh? Really?
HENDEN.   ... has — what? — permits the concept of ... cyclism, I suppose it could be called....
GERTRUDE.   *(Fingertips to temples.)* Stop it, Henden.
HENDEN.   What? Oh.
EDMEE.   *(Fergus is listening, unbeknownst etc. After a tiny pause.)*

It's that Fergus is ... *so* bright I worry for him. Oh, a mother with a dumb one has her own problems — can he find his way *home?* Won't he be embarrassed to be in the third grade at fourteen? Whatever will he *do* with his *life?* Those *are* problems, and I don't envy a woman who *has* them. But Fergus is ready for college and he's just sixteen. We're going to Europe for a year, to Rome, to Athens, to Dendura, to Istanbul, to let him see it all, begin to relate time to place, fact to theory.

GERTRUDE.   Isn't that nice.

EDMEE.   You *still* don't think he's my son, *do* you!

HENDEN.   *(Admonishingly.)* Why, Gertrude!

GERTRUDE.   *(Too innocent by far.)* I didn't say a word! I haven't said a word for ... minutes.

EDMEE.   *(Hard.)* He's not my type, lady! I *told* you that!

GERTRUDE.   I didn't say a word!

HENDEN.   *(To placate.)* What a nice boy he is! *(Fergus turns, pauses, exits just before the end of Edmee's next speech.)*

EDMEE.   You know what bothers me most about him, about Fergus — being so special, being so ... bright, so beautiful and bright? That he'll turn out ... less than he promises. I don't want to be around when his hair recedes or his body starts its way to fat; I don't want to see the expression in his eyes when he looks at his life and sees it's not going to be quite what it might have been. Tarnish! That's what I don't want to see ... tarnish.

GERTRUDE.   *(Cold; to comfort and destroy.)* Well, maybe he'll die young.

EDMEE.   *(Wistful.)* Maybe.

GERTRUDE.   Or maybe you won't be around.

EDMEE.   *(Ibid.)* Maybe.

HENDEN.   Or, or maybe none of that will happen; maybe he'll ... *be* ... everything he might.

EDMEE.   *(Ibid.)* Maybe.

GERTRUDE.   *(Caught up in it.)* My goodness! Wouldn't that be something!

EDMEE.   Yes. Wouldn't it.

SCENE 17

Daniel and Henden, together, Henden arriving.

DANIEL. Hi, Dad.

HENDEN. Hello, son. *(Pause.)*

DANIEL. You should keep your head covered.

HENDEN. Oh?

DANIEL. Burn.

HENDEN. *Aha! (Pause.)*

DANIEL. Cordelia's over there.

HENDEN. I see; I see she is. *(Pause.)* Gertrude's over there.

DANIEL. Yes; I saw.

HENDEN. *Aha. (Pause.)* How is it going?

DANIEL. What?

HENDEN. It! You, Cordelia, Benjamin, what's-her-name, and all that?

DANIEL. "All that?"

HENDEN. *All* right!! *(Pause.)*

DANIEL. *(Shrugs.)* Not bad.

HENDEN. Good?

DANIEL. *(Harder.)* Not *bad. (Pause.)*

HENDEN. Do you want to talk about it?

DANIEL. You *know* better. *(Pause.)*

HENDEN. I am your father....

DANIEL. *(Explodes.)* Christ! Great, suffering Jesus, do we have to go *on* with this?

HENDEN. *(Hurriedly; mollifying.)* No, no, no, no, now ...

DANIEL. *(Continuing.) Must* we go on with it? There is no hope! There is ... going *on;* there is ... getting through it!

HENDEN. *(Softly.)* All *right.*

DANIEL. *(Continuing.)* There is my *nature* and *Benjamin's* nature, and we are doing what we *can* about it, though I think we're *idiots.* We have fallen between stools, Father; we were better perched on our specialness ... our disgrace, perhaps. Perhaps not. I don't know — the perch, I mean; not the specialness. I don't know.

HENDEN. I know.

DANIEL. *(Ironic.)* But we are *trying.* Jesus, we're trying!! Benjamin is heartbroken and confused; Abigail — what's-her-name to you — Abigail is close to a collapse of *some* sort; Cordelia is turning tough and brittle at the same time and is beginning to drink just a little too much, though maybe that's *in* her; and *I* ... *I* can't keep my hands from shaking, *or* shouting at you, dearest man, whom I love above all creatures on this earth. *(Pause.)*

HENDEN. Well.

DANIEL. Yes; well. *(Pause. They embrace; Daniel seems to sob; Henden tentatively hugs him, pats him on the back; they separate, go in opposite directions.)*

SCENE 18

Abigail and Edmee. Edmee seated next to a sleeping Gertrude; Abigail approaches.

ABIGAIL. May we talk?

EDMEE. I suppose we *could;* I don't really *want* to.

ABIGAIL. *(About to leave; shy.)* I'm sorry.

EDMEE. *(Removing her dark glasses.)* No! *I* am! I'm being rude.

ABIGAIL. Well, a little.

EDMEE. *(None too pleasant.)* I like candor in a girl; next to bitten fingernails, I like candor best.

ABIGAIL. *(Looks to be sure.)* I don't bite my nails.

EDMEE. *(Expansive.)* I don't know what it is about the sea — the beach and the sea: they bring out in me a tristesse I feel no other place. It's not a lugubrious sadness or a grief; no, I described it as I intended.

ABIGAIL. A tristesse?

EDMEE. Yes. I have felt fear in the plains, panic in a church, claustrophobia in the mountains, tearing loss at Christmas with all my lovlies around me, implausible sadness on a summer day, but only here, where the earth and water meet, do I feel this ... tristesse.

ABIGAIL.   *(Shy.)* I see.

EDMEE.   We have so much to be thankful for, being alive. *Being alive!!* for one! I've never taken much comfort from "what lies beyond," as they put it. I *doubt* it; I doubt the entire proposition, but even if it does ... occur, the reports are none too encouraging — hellfire for the wicked and a kind of disembodied cloud sit for the rest? What comfort there! What! No dry martinis? No poetry? No ... no whatever makes it all worth the effort? Perhaps I could accept an eternity of tristesse, sitting here with a magazine, my mind, and some memories. *(Turns to Gertrude.)* Are you asleep, my dear?

ABIGAIL.   *(Wistful; lost.)* The water is ... lovely.

EDMEE.   It's the line where it meets; that's the magic! One element into another, *(Snaps her fingers.)* Just like that! I would love to be able to walk into it — the water — walk down the grade, enter, submerge, walk about, reverse and march right back to my starting point, all erect, all ... gliding. I would love to be able to breathe both water and air.

ABIGAIL.   We can ... in a way.

EDMEE.   *(Scoffing.)* Oh, masks and tanks and things!

ABIGAIL.   No; not really. *(Begins to move away.)* Thank you; I enjoyed our talk.

EDMEE.   *(To Gertrude's sleeping form.)* Gertrude? *(To the retreating Abigail.)* Oh! Oh, so did I! I hope I was some ... *(To herself.)* Well, I hope I was some help.

SCENE 19

Abigail and Benjamin. Abigail returning.

BENJAMIN.   *(Casual.)* Where have you been?

ABIGAIL.   Where have *you* been?

BENJAMIN.   Nowhere.

ABIGAIL.   Me, too.

BENJAMIN.   Who were you *talking* to?

ABIGAIL. *(Indicates.)* That lady.

BENJAMIN. Her son is called Fergus; he's ...

ABIGAIL. *(She can't help it.)* ... a little young for you, don't you think?

BENJAMIN. Oh, come *on!* Jesus, can't we even *talk?*

ABIGAIL. I'm sorry! *(Softer.)* I *am;* I'm sorry.

BENJAMIN. *(Taking her hand.)* How can your *hand* be so *cold?* It's hot out here; how can your hand be so cold?

ABIGAIL. *(Withdrawing her hand.)* I'm always cold; I get colder all the time. If you ever held me anymore you'd know.

BENJAMIN. *I* hold you.

ABIGAIL. Sure!

BENJAMIN. *(Anger rising.)* I *hold* you!

ABIGAIL. *(A burst of self-propelled anger.)* Yes! *You* hold me! But I hardly know it's *you,* and who are you holding *really,* and why do you want to hurt me in bed, and why are you walking away, and ... *(Benjamin goes.)* ... and why am I so cold all the time? ... And *(Raises her hand to the sun; slow, quiet intensity now.)* Why don't you just ... go out? Burn out? Flare up, sizzle, crackle for a moment, and then ... just ... fade ... bring the ice down on all of us? *I'm* ready; *I'm* cold enough. Go out! I dare you! *(Pause; pain.)* Benjamin! Benjamin! *(At the end of this scene, and as Scene 20 begins, Abigail takes her towel and exits; none of the others see her exit.)*

SCENE 20

Edmee, Gertrude, and Henden in their chairs.

GERTRUDE. *(Waking up; an announcement of subject.)* Am I asleep, my dear.

EDMEE. *(Pleased.)* Aha!

GERTRUDE. Where is Henden?

HENDEN. *(Eyes closed; hat over his face.)* Asleep, my dear.

GERTRUDE. Aha. *(To Edmee.)* I doze; I slip off into sleepettes. Is it tiny strokes, I wonder — the sleepettes? I will

33

be at a dinner party, attentive to my neighbor, and all at once I am aware I have slipped off for a moment. Or I am reading and it will happen. Tiny strokes? Probably not: Simply that I don't sleep much at night; I cat-prowl. Henden and I still have the same room — the same bed! — and he lies there, a wheezing lump, unconscious.

HENDEN.   Ah, now ...

EDMEE.   *(Literally.)* Tee-hee!

GERTRUDE.   ... and I am awake, almost all the night, dozing fitfully until I am awakened by a creak, a chirp, the memory of a dream.

EDMEE.   *I've* done it.

GERTRUDE.   I do it as clockwork. I am as familiar with dawn as any farmer, the night as any watchman. I waxed the library table once at three in the A.M. down on my knees in my nightdress doing away at the big claw feet.

HENDEN.   Looked grand when you were done. *(Edmee laughs.)*

GERTRUDE.   And I write long letters in the night — wise, instructive, useful — to our leaders, but I seldom mail them: might change the world; wouldn't do — let bad enough alone.

EDMEE.   I sleep without moving.

GERTRUDE.   *(Too bright.)* Who *tells* you?

EDMEE.   *(Smooth.)* Oh ... whoever is with me. I have a ... variety of gentlemen, and one lady, share my night times. I outsleep them; they tell me.

GERTRUDE.   Why did you wonder if I was awake?

EDMEE.   *(Mildly corrective.)* I wondered if you were *asleep.*

GERTRUDE.   Oh. *(Afterthought.)* They are not the same?

HENDEN.   *(Behind his hat.)* Not exactly.

EDMEE.   That ... that girl was talking to me, the young one. I wanted to help.

GERTRUDE.   Abigail?

EDMEE.   Is that her name?

GERTRUDE.   Abigail. She is married to Benjamin. We know all about that.

EDMEE.   Oh?

GERTRUDE.   *(Hurrying through it.)* It's so tedious. Abigail is married by mischance to Benjamin, who by mischance was lovers with Daniel, who by mischance is now married to Cordelia. Cordelia is my daughter, and Daniel is Henden's son.

EDMEE.   Goodness!

GERTRUDE.   *(Waving it all away.)* They travel in a pack; they are not happy! They worry and bother us.

EDMEE.   Gracious!

GERTRUDE.   ... though we have given up trying to solve it all: too much fate; too much irony.

HENDEN.   *I* try ... now and again.

GERTRUDE.   To any end?

HENDEN.   You know better.

EDMEE.   Perhaps it will all resolve itself. I wonder what she wanted.

GERTRUDE.   *(Shrugs.)* To whine; to explain; to be comforted; to save her soul. Who knows? Perhaps it will all resolve itself? Yes; well, perhaps; and — then again — perhaps not. And so ... Henden sleeps and I prowl.

EDMEE.   Jack Sprat!

GERTRUDE.   *(Laughs.)* Yes; in a way.

HENDEN.   Jack who?

GERTRUDE.   Go back to sleep. *(Gertrude and Edmee laugh, sadly gaily.)*

SCENE 21

Benjamin, Cordelia, Daniel, Edmee and Gertrude. Daniel and Cordelia are R., Edmee and Gertrude in their chairs L. Henden is in his chair, back to front.

BENJAMIN.   *(Comes down to Cordelia and Daniel.)* Hold me, you guys.

DANIEL.   Another bout?

BENJAMIN.   *(Still standing.)* Just hold me.

DANIEL.   Come in between.

35

CORDELIA. *(Shrugs; smiles.)* Why not? *(The sun goes behind a cloud; the sky becomes gray.)*
GERTRUDE. *(To Edmee.)* Are we losing the sun?
EDMEE. Hm?
GERTRUDE. I said ...
EDMEE. Why, I think we are.
BENJAMIN. There are days when I just don't ...
DANIEL. Forget it.
BENJAMIN. Why is the sun going away?
DANIEL. *(Sad laugh.)* It's one of those *days.*
BENJAMIN. *(A child.)* What if it were to ... go out?
CORDELIA. That'd solve a few things.
DANIEL. It sure would. *(Sighs.)*
GERTRUDE. *(About the sun.)* Awwwwwwwww.
EDMEE. So much for skin cancer.
GERTRUDE. *(Cheerful.)* Oh, it'll come back.
EDMEE. You and I should talk about facelift sometime.
BENJAMIN. Let well enough alone, I tell her.
CORDELIA. *Well* enough?
DANIEL. Indeed.
BENJAMIN. What?
DANIEL. Let bad enough alone, you mean?
BENJAMIN. Something like that.
GERTRUDE. *(To Edmee.)* Whatever for? Are you planning one?
EDMEE. One likes to think ahead.
GERTRUDE. *I* have the skin of a turtle. *I* don't bother.
BENJAMIN. She says I hurt her in bed.
CORDELIA. *(Gleeful interest.)* Oh? Really?
DANIEL. *(Chuckles.)* Down, girl!
EDMEE. If you're as vain as I am, then you look around the next corner.
GERTRUDE. *(A bit chiding, a bit taunting.)* What would your Fergie say?
EDMEE. *(Laughs.)* Well, then your dreams might come *true.* *(Offhand.)* Where *is* he, I wonder?
BENJAMIN. I think one day it'll have to be just ... the three of us.

36

CORDELIA.   Only if you'll promise to hurt me.

DANIEL.   He'll find a way — one way or another.

BENJAMIN.   *I'm* gentle. How about it, guys? The three of us?

CORDELIA.   The *two* of you, you mean.

DANIEL.   Oh, come on, baby!

CORDELIA.   I'll bow *out;* I *will.*

GERTRUDE.   *(To Edmee.)* Do you think I *should* have it done?

EDMEE.   Couldn't hurt.

GERTRUDE.   I wonder what Henden would say?

EDMEE.   Ask him.

GERTRUDE.   *(Looks.)* He's asleep. He probably wouldn't notice.

BENJAMIN.   The musketeers.

CORDELIA.   *(Looking.)* There's a crowd down there at the water.

DANIEL.   A whale, probably; a shark.

CORDELIA.   *(Puzzled frown.)* No; no, I don't think so.

DANIEL.   Well, why don't you go *see?*

CORDELIA.   *(Rising, moving off.)* Yes. Yes, I think I will. *(Exits.)*

DANIEL.   *(Imitation of a witch.)* Now we're alone, baby!

BENJAMIN.   *(Sincere.)* Oh, Daniel; hold me. *(Daniel does, gently.)*

EDMEE.   There would appear to be two theories about facelift — at least! One is, wait until you're nicely lined and sagged and wattled, and *then* do it. The *other* is, do it often and surreptitiously — never look a day older than when you've begun it.

GERTRUDE.   Our skin ages, no matter what you do.

EDMEE.   Oh, you have to stay out of the sun.

GERTRUDE.   Stay out of the sun!? Are you mad!?

EDMEE.   *(Chuckles; then.)* There are *people* down there.

GERTRUDE.   *(Not interested.)* Oh? *(Intense.)* Why doesn't the sun come back?

BENJAMIN.   Do we have to go on this way? Can't we go back to how we were?

DANIEL.   I don't think so.

BENJAMIN.   I *love* you; you love *me*. I don't hurt *you*.

DANIEL.   No; we can't.

BENJAMIN.   We could *try*.

DANIEL.   What do you want to do with the girls? Grow up!

BENJAMIN.   I *miss* you.

DANIEL.   *(Pause.)* I miss *you*.

BENJAMIN.   I *love* you.

DANIEL.   *(Pause.)* I love *you?*

GERTRUDE.   Henden?

EDMEE.   Let him sleep.

BENJAMIN.   It's hope-less, then.

DANIEL.   It's hopeless, then. What did Beckett say?: I can't go on; I'll go on?

GERTRUDE.   Henden? *(Cordelia returns with Abigail's towel.)*

BENJAMIN.   *(Puzzled.)* That's Abigail's towel.

CORDELIA.   No beached whale; no shark.

BENJAMIN.   That's Abigail's!

DANIEL.   *(Eyes narrowing.)* What's wrong?

CORDELIA.   *(Looking back toward the water.)* Abigail tried to drown herself. They stopped her. They have her over a bar-rel — literally; they're pumping the water out of her. She'll live. *(Tosses the towel to Benjamin.)* Here; this belongs to you.

BENJAMIN.   *(Awe; not moving.)* She tried to drown herself? Why?

DANIEL.   *(He and Cordelia chuckle sadly.)* Oh, God.

GERTRUDE.   Henden?

BENJAMIN.   *(Generally.)* *Hold* me?

EDMEE.   Let him *sleep*.

GERTRUDE.   *(Senses something.)* Henden! *(Goes to his chair.)* Henden?

EDMEE.   Let him ... *(She, too, realizes.)* Is he dead?

GERTRUDE.   *(Long pause.)* Yes; yes, he is.

EDMEE.   Poor him; poor *you*.

GERTRUDE.   Poor Henden; poor, dear man.

EDMEE.   *(Quiet panic.)* Fergus!

BENJAMIN.   *(Not moving.)* I'll have to go to her.

CORDELIA.   Let them wring her out. What would you say to her?

BENJAMIN. *(Pause.)* Nothing?

GERTRUDE. *(To Daniel, from where she is.)* Daniel?

DANIEL. *(Pause; soft.)* Yes, Gertrude?

GERTRUDE. You'd better come here.

EDMEE. Fergus?

DANIEL. Is it my father?

GERTRUDE. You know. Yes.

EDMEE. Fergus?

DANIEL. I'll come in a moment.

CORDELIA. Oh, Daniel, poor Daniel.

EDMEE. Fergus?

BENJAMIN. Hold me?

DANIEL. *(Gently.)* Oh, God.

GERTRUDE. Oh, Henden.

EDMEE. Fergus!!?

BENJAMIN. *Hold me!? Someone!?*

CORDELIA. Anyone? Here. *(Holds him.)*

EDMEE. Fergus?

GERTRUDE. Oh, my poor Henden.

DANIEL. Oh, God.

EDMEE. *(A frightened child.)* Fergus?

GERTRUDE. He'll come back, my dear; they do. Look! The sun's returning. What glory! What ... wonder! *(Indeed, the sun is returning.)*

BENJAMIN. Daniel?

EDMEE. Fergus?

GERTRUDE. Oh, my Henden.

DANIEL. Oh, God.

EDMEE. Fergus? *(Pause.)* Fergus? *(Pause; slow fade.)*

END

NEW
PLAYS

LONELY PLANET
by Steven Dietz

THE AMERICA PLAY
by Suzan-Lori Parks

THE FOURTH WALL
by A.R. Gurney

JULIE JOHNSON
by Wendy Hammond

FOUR DOGS AND A BONE
by John Patrick Shanley

DESDEMONA, A PLAY ABOUT A
HANDKERCHIEF
by Paula Vogel

*Write for information as to
availability*
DRAMATISTS PLAY SERVICE, Inc.
440 Park Avenue South   New York, N.Y. 10016